THE
ZEN
BOOK OF LIFE

THE
ZEN
BOOK OF LIFE

WISDOM FROM THE GREAT MASTERS, TEACHERS, AND WRITERS OF ALL TIME

MARK ZOCCHI

HAMPTON ROADS

Cover artwork: "The Red Dance," watercolour and guache.
© Tim Hayward. Private Collection/Bridgeman Images
Illustrations by Mark Zocchi, and other select stock sources.
Cover and interior design by Kathryn Sky-Peck
Typeset in Weiss

Hampton Roads Publishing Company, Inc.
Charlottesville, VA 22906
Distributed by Red Wheel/Weiser, LLC
www.redwheelweiser.com
Sign up for our newsletter and special offers by going to
www.redwheelweiser.com/newsletter.

ISBN: 978-1-64297-004-3
Library of Congress Cataloging-in-Publication Data available upon request.

Printed in Canada
MAR

10 9 8 7 6 5 4 3 2 1

INTRODUCTION

Inspired by the Buddha and the great Zen masters, the intention of this little book is to help awaken the reader's own wisdom mind.

The Zen Book of Life is filled with quotes, Haiku (Zen Poems) and Koans (traditional riddles that a master asks a student to inspire the student's awakening).

Zen is a school of Buddhism that arose in China around the fourth century CE but was refined in Japan when a South Indian Buddhist monk named Bodhidharma allegedly brought the "mind only" teaching there and started a lineage.

There is one teaching that is thought to be central to Zen. One day the Buddha was to give a teaching to huge assembly of monks and nuns gathered. The Buddha did not speak but simply held up a flower. The crowd became restless and eager for the Buddha's teaching to begin. But a senior disciple, Kashaya, only smiled. The Buddha said Kashaya had understood the teaching and was to be known from then on as Mahakashyapa.

Mahakashyapa understood the highest wisdom of the Buddha. In that moment of the Buddha holding up the flower a direct mind-to-mind transmission had occurred and this is seen as the beginning of the Zen lineage.

Typically Zen is a direct approach where Haiku and Koan are used to break conceptual thinking leading to a glimpse of satori or enlightenment.

This direct teaching or wisdom teaching is known as Zen, Chaun in Chinese and Dzogchen in Tibetan.

Any attempt to describe Zen in words will fall short, because they are words and not the experience of Zen. Or as one Zen master said, "The finger pointing to the moon is not the moon." However the blessing of the finger pointing to the moon is that it helps turn our focus in the right direction.

May *The Zen Book of Life* help turn your mind to uncover your own wisdom.

ZEN WISDOM

Zen in its essence

is the art of seeing

into the nature of one's being,

and it points the way

from bondage to freedom.

D.T. SUZUKI

Although I try to hold
the single thought
Of Buddha's teaching in my heart,
I cannot help but hear the many
crickets' voices calling as well.

ISUMI SHIKIBU

We accept the graceful falling
Of mountain cherry blossoms,
But it is much harder for us
To fall away from our own
Attachment to the world

ZEN WISDOM

When my house burned down

I gained

An unobstructed view

of the moonlight sky

ZEN WISDOM

Out of clutter,

find simplicity.

From discord,

find harmony.

In the middle of difficulty

lies opportunity.

ALBERT EINSTEIN

With plum blossom scent,
This sudden sun emerges
Along a mountain trail

BASHO

You the butterfly–
I, Chuang Tzu's
dreaming heart.

It is not difficult to keep

a beginners mind.

There are many possibilities

in a beginners mind,

but in the expert few.

SUSKI ROSHI

Zen is simply . . .

That state of centeredness

which is here and now.

ALAN WATTS

The world?
Moonlit water drops
From the crane's bill

ZEN MASTER DOGEN

See the world through your Heart.

MZ

What delight it is

When I blow away ash,

To watch the crimson

Of the glowing fire

And hear the water boil.

TACHIBANA AKEMI

Sit quietly doing nothing,

Spring comes,

And the grass grows

By itself.

ZEN WISDOM (SAYING)

Meditating deeply
Reach the depth of the source.
Branching streams cannot compare
to this source.
Sitting alone in a great silence,
even though the heavens turn
and the earth is upset,
you will not even blink

NYOGEN SENZAKI

There is no place in Buddhism for using effort.
Just be ordinary and nothing special.
Relieve your bowels, pass water,
Put your clothes on
and eat your food.
Ignorant people will laugh at me,
But wise will understand.

LIN-CHI

Refraining from all evil,
Not clinging to birth and death,
Working with deep compassion
for all sentient beings,
respecting those over you
and pitying those below you,
with out any detesting or desiring,
worrying or lamentation—
This is what is called Buddha
Do not Search beyond it.

ZEN MASTER DOGEN

The resting place for the mind is the heart

BUDDHIST MONK

Do not seek the truth.
Only cease to cherish options.

ZEN SAYING

If we speak of what is real

Even a speck of dust

or grain of sand is real

Yet nothing is real

Everything is illusory

Like the moon reflected in water

Neither real or unreal

is the infinite void

ZEN POEM, VIETNAMESE BUDDHIST MONK

Everything that begins also ends.

Make peace with that and all will be well.

THE BUDDHA

Zen mind is not Zen mind
That is,
if you are attached to Zen mind,
Then you have a problem,
And your way is very narrow.
Throwing away Zen mind
is correct Zen mind.
Only keeping the question,
What is the best way of helping
other people?

SEUNG SAHN

To be enlightened is to be intimate with all things

ZEN MASTER DOGEN

One who excels in travelling

Leaves no tracks.

One who excels as a warrior

Does not appear formidable.

One who excels in fighting

Is never aroused by anger.

One who excels in employing others

Humbles himself before them.

ZEN TRADITION

To see a World in a Grain of Sand

And a Heaven in a Wild Flower.

Hold infinity in the palm of your hand

And Eternity in an hour

WILLIAM BLAKE

The Zen of doing anything is doing with a particular concentration of mind, a calmness and simplicity of mind that brings the experience of enlightenment and, through that experience happiness.

D. T. SUZUKI

All that we are is the result
of what we have thought.
It is founded on our thoughts,
It is made up of our thoughts

THE DHAMMAPADA

There is nothing good or bad,
but thinking makes it so.

WILLIAM SHAKESPEARE

Ask not what tomorrow may bring

But count as blessing

Every day that fate allows you.

HORACE

Every Day is a good day.

UNMON

Every thing comes at its appointed time

I CHING

Do not dwell in the past

Do not dream of the future.

Concentrate the mind

On the present moment.

THE BUDDHA

If you really know how to live,
what better way to start the day
than with a smile?
Smiling helps you approach the day
with gentleness and understanding.
Smile with your whole being.

THICH NHAT HANH

The Universe doesn't make mistakes

CHRIS PRENTISS

We are here and it is now.
Further than that all
human knowledge
Is moonshine.

H.L. MENCKEN

Your worst enemy cannot harm you
As much as your own thoughts,
unguarded.
But once mastered,
No one can help you as much.

THE DHAMMAPADA

Think with your whole body

TAISEN DESHIMARU

Meditating deeply…
Reach the depth of the source.
Branching streams
Cannot compare to this source!
Sitting alone in a great silence,
He who binds to himself a joy
Does the winged life destroy;
But he who kisses joy as it flies
Lives in Eternity sunrise.

WILLIAM BLAKE

Out of eternity

The new day is born

Into eternity at night will return.

THOMAS CARLYLE

When you arise in the morning

Give thanks for the morning light.

Give thanks for life and strength.

Give thanks for your food.

And give thanks for the joy of living.

And if perchance you see no reason to give thanks

Rest assured the fault is yours.

AMERICAN INDIAN SAYING

Even if it is painful and lonely
associate with worthy companions

ZEN MASTER DOGEN

To see the things of the present moment
Is to see all that is now,
All that has been since time began,
And all that shall be unto the world's end;
For all things are of
One kind and one form

MARCUS AURELIUS

The sage blends everything into a
harmonious whole. He is unmindful
of the confusion and the gloom,
and equalizes the humble and the
honourable.

CHUANG TZU

Everything that happens to us is for
our complete benefit.

CHRIS PRENTISS

The only way to make sense out of
change is to plunge with it, move
with it, and join in the dance.

ALAN WATTS

Dew-drops—
how better wash away
world's dust?

He who has once known contentment

The contentment that

Comes simply through being content

Will never again be otherwise than contented.

TAO TE CHING

To find perfect composure in the midst of change
is to find nirvana

SHUNRYU SUZUKI ROSHI

When you can be calm
in the midst of activity,
This is the true state of nature…
When you can be happy
in the midst of hardship,
then you see the true potential of the mind

HAUCHU DAOREN

If you laugh at misfortune,
you will not be overcome by it.

VALLUVAR

Know all things like this
A mirage, a cloud castle
Nothing appears as it is.

THE BUDDHA

The universe always strikes you at
your weakest point
Because that's what needs most
strengthening

CHRIS PRENTISS

We accept the graceful falling
Of mountain cherry blossoms,
But it is much harder for us
To fall away from our own
Attachment to the world

ZEN WISDOM

The miracle is not to fly in the air or walk on water,
but to walk on the earth

CHINESE PROVERB

Do not pursue the past

Do not lose your self in the future

The past no longer is.

The future is yet to come.

Looking very deeply at life as it is

here and now;

The practitioner dwells in stability and freedom

BHADDEKARATTA SUTTA

The present moment is a wonderful moment

THICH NHAT HANH

If the mind is never aroused toward objects,
Then wherever you walk is the site of enlightenment

POA-CHIH

Never say "cannot" for you are infinite
Even time and space are as nothing compared
With your nature.
You can do anything

SWAMI VIVEKANANDA

Live life Abundantly
This is why you have it.
Don't fear, don't contract,
Open and enjoy.

MZ

The Birds have vanished into the sky
And now the last cloud fades away.
We sit together, the mountain and I,
Until only the mountain remains

LI PO

To abandon what is harmful,

To adopt what is wholesome,

To purify the heart and mind:

This is the teaching of the Buddha.

THE BUDDHA

If you want to be happy,

Be.

TOLSTOY

The Only truth you find at the top of the mountain
Is the truth you brought with you.

ZEN SAYING

The gap between what is and what
"should be" is an ocean of distress.

CHRISTINA FELDMAN

I have three things to teach;

Simplicity, patience and compassion,

These three are your great treasures,

Simple actions and in thought,

You return to the source of being,

Patience with both friends and enemies,

You accord with the way things are,

Compassionate toward yourself,

You reconcile all beings in the world.

TAO TE CHING

Contentment is the great elixir

SOGYAL RINPOCHE

Breathing in, I calm my body,

Breathing out, I smile.

Dwelling in the present moment

I know this a wonderful moment.

THICH NHAT HANH

If you are in the moment,

you are in the infinite.

SVAMI PRAJNANPAD

Of what avail is it if we can travel
to the moon,
If we cannot cross the abyss that
separates us from ourselves,
This is the most important of all journeys
And without it all of the rest are useless

THOMAS MERTON

The enlightened person is not
exempt from any form
Of feelings but is not bound or
governed by them.
The arrow will hurt, but the pain of
the body will not be matched by the
sorrow and struggle in the mind.

CHRISTINA FELDMAN

Within your own house swells the treasure of joy,
So why do you go begging from door to door?

Surrendering the story is not a dismissal of the wounded leg, but an empowerment, releasing the capacity to care for what needs to be cared for with compassion and responsiveness, letting go of all the extra layers of fear, apprehension, and blame.

CHRISTINA FELDMAN

In the pursuit of knowledge,
every day something is gained.
In the pursuit of freedom,
everyday something is let go.

TAO TE CHING

Renunciation is not getting rid of
things of this world,
But accepting that they pass away

ROBERT AITKEN ROSHI

Practicing meditation is to be aware,
to smile, to breathe.

THICH NHAT HANH

When you walk, just walk.

When you sit, just sit.

Just be your ordinary natural self

in ordinary life, unconcerned in seeking

for Buddhahood.

When you're tired, lie down.

The fool will laugh at you

but the wise man will understand.

LIN CHI

How I long to see
among dawn flowers,
the face of God.

What is this moment lacking?

ZEN QUESTION

No one who truly loves themselves
would harm another,
For they would be harming themselves.

THE BUDDHA

Everyone sooner or later,
Sits down to a basket of consequences

ROBERT LOUIS STEVENSON

Long accustomed to contemplating compassion,
I no longer see a difference between myself and other.

MILAREPA

The body is the bodhi tree
The mind a mirror bright,
Carefully we polish them hour by hour,
And let no dust alight.

There is no bodhi tree,
Nor is there mirror bright,
Buddha nature shines clear and bright,
Where can dust alight

HUI NENG

Better than a thousand careless words
is one single word that gives peace.
Better than a hundred years lived heedlessness,
Without contemplation,
Is one single day lived in wisdom
and deep contemplation.
Better than a hundred years lived in confusion,
Is a single day lived with courage and wise intention.

THE DHAMMAPADA

Nothing can do us more harm than
a thought unguarded
But once understood there is nothing
that can be a greater friend,
Not even your father and mother.

THE BUDDHA

The universe is change,
our life is what our thoughts make it.

MARCUS AURELIUS

Earth brings us to life
and nourishes us.
Earth takes us back again.
Birth and death are present
in every moment.

THICH NHAT HANH

Death is extraordinary like life,
when we know how to live.
You cannot live without dying.
You cannot live if you do not die
psychologically every minute.

KRISHNAMURTI

When we begin to practice the basic meditation of tranquillity meditation [shamatha], we may find that our mind won't stay still for a moment. But this condition is not permanent and will change as we practice. Eventually we will be able to place our mind at rest at will, at which point we will have successfully alleviated the manifest disturbance of the disturbing emotions. After developing tranquillity meditation, we can then apply the second technique, of insight meditation [vipashyana], which consists of learning to recognise and directly experience the nature of our own mind. This nature is referred to as emptiness. When we recognise this nature, and rest in it, then all of the disturbing emotions that arise dissolve into this emptiness and are no longer afflictions. This is the freedom, which is called Buddhahood.

KHENCHEN THRANGU RINPOCHE

I'd rather be happy than right.

RAM DASS

Out behind the ideas of wrongdoing and right doing

There is a field, I'll meet you there,

When the soul lies down in that grass,

The world is too full to talk about

Ideas, language, even the phrase

"each other"

Does not make sense

RUMI

If you want to know what compassion is,

Look into the eyes of a mother as

She cradles her fevered, ill child.

THE BUDDHA

The fundamental delusion of humanity

is to suppose that I am here and you are out there.

HAKUUN YASUTANI ROSHI

We cannot always fix every
event distress,
But can always be present, awake,
and receive each moment with
compassion and simplicity.

CHRISTINA FELDMAN

The only lasting beauty
is beauty of the heart.

RUMI

I am unable to restrain external things,

but I shall restrain my own mind.

What need is there to restrain anything else?

SHANTIDEVA

Mindfulness is a shortcut to happiness.

BUDDHIST MONK

Enlightenment is like the
moon reflected on the water,
The moon does not get wet,
nor is the water broken.
Although its light is wide and great
The moon is reflected even by
a puddle an inch wide,
The whole moon and the entire sky
are reflected in one dew drop
on the grass.

ZEN MASTER DOGEN

The Real voyage of discovery lies not
in finding new landscapes,
But in having new eyes.

MARCEL PROUST

In this moment what is lacking.

ZEN SAYING

Learn to be happy, here and now,
under all conditions; and to include
others' happiness in your own joy.
Go out of your way to make others happy.

PARAMAHANSA YOGANANDA

Learning to meditate is the greatest gift
you can give yourself in this life.

SOGYAL RINPOCHE

If the inner mind has been tamed,
the outer enemy cannot harm you.

ATISA

What life can compare with this?
Sitting quietly by the window,
I watch leaves fall and the flowers bloom
as the seasons come and go.

SECCHO

Not thinking about anything is Zen.

Once you know this, walking, standing,

sitting or lying down, everything you do is Zen.

To know that the mind is empty is to see the Buddha.

Using the mind to look for reality is delusion.

Not using the mind to look for reality

is awareness.

Freeing yourself from words is liberation.

BODHIDHARMA

Such fragrance—
from where?
which tree?

Act without acting on.
Work without working at.

LAO TZU

When sitting, sit;
when standing, stand.
Above all, don't wobble.

ZEN SAYING

We are what we think.

All that we are arises with our thoughts.

With our thoughts we make the world.

Speak or act with an impure mind

and trouble will follow you.

As the wheel follows the ox that draws the cart.

We are what we think.

All that we are arises with our thoughts.

With our thoughts we made the world.

Speak or act with a pure mind

and happiness will follow you

As your shadow unshakeable.

THE DHAMMAPADA

To a sincere student,
Every day is a fortunate day

SUZUKI ROSHI

The foolish reject what they see;
The wise reject what they think.

ZEN SAYING

Obey the nature of things and
you will walk freely and undisturbed

SENG-TS'AN

The truth is always near at hand,
within your reach.

D.T. SUZUKI

The whole world is a door of liberation,
inviting us to enter.

ZEN SAYING

When anger rises,
think of the consequences.

CONFUCIUS

If you are patient in one moment of anger,
you will escape a hundred days of sorrow.

CHINESE PROVERB

Write in your heart
That every day
Is the best day of the year

RALPH WALDO EMERSON

The highest nobility lies in taming your own mind

ATHISA

Come, see real
flowers
of this painful world.

Take time to listen to

what is not said without words

To obey the law too subtle to be written

To worship the unnameable,

And to embrace the unformed

LAO TZU

To breathe out, let go of the story,
And find the generosity to be
wholeheartedly present

CHRISTINA FELDMAN

Fragrance always clings to the hand
that gives you roses.

CHINESE PROVERB

It is easier to go up the hill than down,
But the view is from the top.

ARNOLD BENNETT

There are no ordinary moments.

DAN MILLMAN

As soon as you have made a thought, laugh at it.

LAO TZU

From the withered tree the flower blooms.

SHOYO ROKO

This zendo is not a peaceful haven
but a furnace room for combustion
of our egotistical delusions.

EIDO ROSHI

To be uncertain is to be uncomfortable,
but to be certain is to be ridiculous.

The three great vices seem to be
efficiency, punctuality, and the desire
for achievement and success.
They are the things that make people so unhappy
and so nervous.

LIN YUTANG

By letting it go it gets all done.

The world is won by those who let it go.

But when you try and try,

the world is beyond the winning.

LAO TZU

Grant yourself a moment of peace and you will understand how foolishly you have scurried about. Learn to be silent and you will notice that you have talked too much.

TSCHEN TSCHI JU

Besides the noble art of getting things done, there is a nobler art of leaving things undone. The wisdom of life consists in the elimination of nonessentials.

LIN YUTANG

All beings are on the path,
all victims of the same existence.
No one is better than the next person.

DENG MING-DAO

When I begin to sit
With the dawn in solitude,
I begin to really live.
It makes me treasure
Every single moment of life

GLORIA VANDERBILT

The best person is like water.

Water is good; it benefits all things

and does not compete with them.

It dwells in lowly places that all disdain.

TAO TE CHING

The softest things in the world
overcome the hardest things in the world.

LAO TZU

The best soldier does not attack.

The superior fighter succeeds without violence.

The greatest conqueror wins without struggle.

The most successful manager leads
without dictating.

FROM THE TAO TE CHING

If you realize that you have enough,

you are truly rich.

FROM THE TAO TE CHING

He who grasps loses.

LAO TZU

So if loss of what gives
happiness causes you
distress when it fades, you
can now understand that
such happiness is worthless.

CHUANG TZU

Summer grasses,

all that remains of soldiers' dreams.

BASHO

Life is a series of natural
and spontaneous changes.
Don't resist them—that only creates sorrow.
Let reality be reality.
Let things flow naturally forward
in whatever way they will.

TAO TE CHING

What the caterpillar calls the end,
the rest of the world calls a butterfly.

LAO TZU

A tree that is unbending is easily broken.

LAO TZU

When I let go of what I am,
I become what I might be.

LAO TZU

Autumn—even
birds and clouds
look old.

Changelessness is death.

CHINESE PROVERB

To be the best person be careful of these things:
Your face that it may always reflect kindness; your
manners that they might show respect for other
people; your words that they may be true; your
dealings with other people that they may be fair.

CONFUCIUS

Kindness in words creates confidence.

Kindness in thinking creates profoundness.

Kindness in giving creates love.

LAO TZU

Manifest plainness, embrace
simplicity, reduce selfishness,
have few desires.

LAO TZU

He who knows he has enough is rich.

TAO TE CHING

Silence is a source of great strength.

LAO TZU

Music in the soul can be heard by the universe.

LAO TZU

To have peace in ones' soul
is the greatest happiness.

ZEN WISDOM

Whenever you hear that someone
else has been successful, rejoice.
Always practice rejoicing for others —
whether your friend or your enemy.
If you cannot practice rejoicing,
no matter how long you live,
you will not be happy.

LAO TZU

We sat together, the forest and I,
merging into silence. Until
only the forest remained.

LI PO

Drinking tea, eating rice, I pass
my time as it comes; looking down at the stream,
looking up at the mountain, how serene and relaxed
I feel indeed!

ZEN POEM

As we do consistent, patient zazen we begin to know that we are nothing but attachments; they rule our lives. But we never lose an attachment by saying it has to go. Only as we gain true awareness of its true nature does it quietly and imperceptibly wither away; like a sandcastle with waves rolling over, it just smoothes out and finally Where is it? What was it?

CHARLOTTE JOKO BECK

To the mind that is still,
the whole universe surrenders.

LAO TZU

We reflect on paradox:

water wears away rock.

Spirit overcomes force.

The weak will undo the mighty.

May we learn to see things backwards,

inside out, and upside down.

LAO TZU

Contemplating the clear moon
Reflecting a mind empty as an open sky
Drawn by beauty, I lose myself
In the shadows it casts.

ZEN MASTER DOGEN

The only way
To make sense out of change
Is to plunge with it
Move with it,
And join the dance.

ALAN WATTS

Outside teaching;
part from tradition.
Not founded on words and letters.
Pointing directly
to the human mind.
Seeing into one's nature
and attaining.

BUDDHAHOOD

If you cant find the truth right where you are,
where else do you expect to find it?

ZEN MASTER DOGEN

Seeing through to essential nature
is the window of enlightenment.

HAKUUN YASUTANI ROSHI

Those with limited views
Are fearful and irresolute,
The faster they hurry,
The slower they go.

SENG-TS'AN

To those who have conformed
Themselves to the Way,
The Way readily Lends its power

TAO TE CHING

We can find ourselves leaning into the
future that has not arrived,
Or leaning back into the past that
has long gone
This is the very moment that we
can calmly stand in the moment
Letting go of our resistance on the
breath and soften our warm hearts

MZ

One who does not grasp hold of
anything is not agitated.
One who is not agitated is close
to freedom.

THE BUDDHA

Every time you smile at someone,
it is an action of love, a gift to that
person, a beautiful thing.

MOTHER THERESA

Stop talking and thinking, then
there is nowhere you cannot go.
Returning to the source,
you gain the meaning; chasing forms, you
lose the wholeness. A moment's
true insight transcends all.

SOSAN

My mind is the guiding-reign

THE BUDDHA

When my heart is at peace,
the world is at peace.

CHINESE PROVERB

Fidelity to grace in my life
is fidelity to simplicity,
rejecting ambition and analysis
and elaborate thought,
or even elaborate concern.
A breath of Zen blows all these cobwebs
out the window.

THOMAS MERTON

Upon goodness of heart
is built wise attention;
Upon wise attention
is built liberating wisdom

THE BUDDHA

The definition of an enlightened person
is that they always have what they need.
Whether sitting alone on a mountain,
Or in the middle of a crowd,
There is no sense of anything absent or lacking.

BAKER ROSHI

Chilling autumn rains
Curtain Mount Fuji, then make it
More beautiful to see

BASHO

Flow with whatever may happen
and let your mind be free:
Stay centered by accepting whatever
you are doing. This is the ultimate.

CHUANG TZU

The quieter you become
The more you are able to hear.

ZEN SAYING

As yesterday is history

And tomorrow may never come,

I have resolved from this day on,

I will do the business I can honestly,

have all the good I can do willingly,

and save my digestion by thinking pleasantly.

ROBERT LOUIS STEVENSON

The true man sees what the eye sees,

and does not add to some thing that

is not there.

He hears what the ears hear

and does not detect imaginary

undertones or overtones.

He is not busy with hidden meaning.

CHUNG TZU

Zen

Is not some kind of excitement,

But merely concentration

On our usual every day life.

SHRUNRYU SUZUKI

Silence is a friend
That will never betray

CONFUCIUS

We are not in chaos
we are the chaos.

MZ

Calming,

Smiling,

Present moment,

Wonderful moment.

THICH NHAT HANH

You must be the change you
wish to see in the world.

MAHATMA GANDHI

Loving what is

BYRON KATIE

The only true strength is
a strength that people do not fear.

LAO TZU

When you're deluded,
every statement is an ulcer;
when you're enlightened,
every word is wisdom.

ZHIQU

No thought, no reflection,
no analysis, no cultivation,
no intention; let it settle itself.

YING-AN

Form is empty of a separate self,
but it is full of everything else in the cosmos.
The same is true with feelings, perceptions,
mental formations, and consciousness.

THICH NHAT HANH

No matter how many years
you sit doing zazen,
you will never become
anything special.

ZEN MASTER SAWAKI

Let your mind wander in simplicity,
blend your spirit with the vastness,
follow along with things the way they are,
and make no room for personal views—
then the world will be governed.

CHUANG-TZU

God has no religion.

MAHATMA GANDHI

All conditioned things are
impermanent.
Work out your own salvation with diligence.

THE BUDDHA'S LAST WORDS

Do not mistake understanding for realisation,
and do not mistaken realisation for liberation.

TIBETAN SAYING

Giving is the first of the six perfections.

Mind is beyond measure.

Things are given beyond measure.

Moreover, in giving, mind transforms

the gift and the gift transforms mind.

ZEN MASTER DOGEN

Day after day the sun.

ZEN SAYING

He who wherever he goes is attached to no person and to no place by ties of flesh; who accepts good and evil alike, neither welcoming the one nor shrinking from the other—take it that such a one has attained Perfection.

BHAGAVAD GITA

Do not speak—unless it improves on silence.

BUDDHIST SAYING

The journey of a thousand miles
must begin with a single step.

LAO TZU

If you understand,
things are just as they are;
if you do not understand,
things are just as they are.

ZEN PROVERB

Your Treasure House is in yourself,
it contains all you need.

HUI HAI

When the pupil is ready to learn,
a teacher will appear.

ZEN PROVERB

Teachers open the door…

You enter by yourself.

CHINESE PROVERB

Before enlightenment:
chop wood, carry water.
After enlightenment:
chop wood, carry water.

OLD ZEN SAYING

We cannot see our reflection in running water.
It is only in still water that we can see.

TAOIST PROVERB

The world is like a mirror.
Smile and your friends smile back.

JAPANESE ZEN SAYING

A flower falls even though
we love it and a weed grows
even though we do not love it.

DOGEN ZENJI

No road to happiness or sorrow…
Find them in yourself.

CHINESE PROVERB

When is the path?
The Zen Master Nan-sen was asked.
Everyday life is the path,
he answered.

MASTER NAN-SEN

If you light a lamp for somebody,
it will also brighten your own path.

BUDDHIST SAYING

We are shaped by our thoughts;
we become what we think.
When the mind is pure,
joy follows like a shadow that never leaves.

THE BUDDHA

It takes a wise man to learn from his mistakes,
but an even wiser man to learn from others.

ZEN PROVERB

Not thinking of good, not thinking of evil—
tell me, what was your original face
before your mother and father were born?

ZEN KOAN

In Zen there is nothing to explain,
Nothing to teach that will add
to your knowledge.
Unless it grows out of yourself,
no knowledge is really of value to you
a borrowed plumage never grows.

D. T. SUZUKI

Zen is expressed simply by sitting

SHUNRYU SUZUKI ROSHI

Living beings are numberless,

I vow to save them all

Confusions are inexhaustible,

I vow to cut them all

Dharma gates are boundless,

I vow to enter them all,

The Buddha-way is unattainable,

I vow to attain it.

BODHISATTVA VOW

The supreme good is like water,

Which nourishes all things without trying to.

LAO TZU

You should practice like your head is on fire.

OLD ZEN SAYING

Softness triumphs over hardness,
Feebleness over strength.
What is more malleable is
always superior over that
which is immovable.

LAO TZU

Anything on the path can be used for realisation.

LO JONG TEACHINGS (TIBETAN TERM)

Try not to localize the mind anywhere,

but let it fill up the whole body,

let it flow throughout the totality of your being.

When this happens, you use your hands

where they are needed, you use your legs and eyes

where they are needed and no time or energy

to waste.

TAKUAN SOHO

(ADVICE TO A YOUNG SAMURAI)

The ear hears sounds but the mind does not move

HUI-NENG
(ON THE ENLIGHTENED MIND)

Mother I knew

Every time I see the ocean

Every time

BASHO

The religion is real living;
living with all one's soul,
with all one's goodness.

ALBERT EINSTEIN

I think of all the places I've been,

Chasing from one famous spot to another,

Who would guess I'd end up

under a pine tree,

Clasping my knees in the

whispering cold?

HAN-SHAN

Illusory dreams, phantom flowers—
Sixty-seven years
A white bird vanishes in the mist,
Autumn waters merge with the sky.

ZEN MASTER HUNG-CHIH

Elements of the Self,
come and go like clouds
without purpose.

ZEN SAYING

If you can rid your self
of conceptual thought,
you will have accomplished everything.

HUANG PO

Trust in things being as
they are is the secret of life.

CHARLOTTE JOKO BECK

Zen is not some fancy,
special art of living,
Our teaching is just to live,
always in reality,
In its exact sense.

SHUNRYU SUZUKI

Life is the way it is.

CHARLOTTE JOKO BECK

Be a lamp unto yourself

THE BUDDHA

There is a task to do, and we just need to do it,
fear or no fear. I struggle with my life because
instead of just doing what needs to needs to be done,
I fight the underlying fear.

CHARLOTTE JOKO BECK

In walking just walk.

In sitting, just sit.

Above all, don't wobble.

YUN-MEN

Anything on the path can be used.

Fear is an illusion

CHARLOTTE JOKO BECK

As a man thinketh in his heart, so is he.

PROVERBS 23:7

be happy, be.

HENRY THOREAU

The Tao is near and people seek it far away.

MENCIUS

I am not ashamed to confess
that I am ignorant
of what I do not know.

CICERO

A man with outward courage
dares to die
A man with inward courage
dares to live.

LAO TZU

There's nothing in the world
so admired as a man
Who knows how to bear
unhappiness with courage.

SENECA

Fear always springs from ignorance.

RALPH WALDO EMERSON

Life is either a daring adventure or nothing.

HELEN KELLER

The universe is change;
our life is what our thoughts
make it.

MARCUS AURELIUS

We are what we think.
All that we are arises
with our thoughts.
With our thoughts
we make the word.

THE BUDDHA

Unhappy with your life,
change your thinking.

MZ

In the World of Reality
there is no self.
There is no other-than-self.

SENG-T'SAN

Attachment is the greatest
fabricator of illusions;
reality can be attained only
by someone who is detached.

SIMONE WEIL

The words of truth
are always paradoxical.

LAO TZU

Form is emptiness,

and the very emptiness is form;

Emptiness does not differ from form,

form does not differ from emptiness;

Whatever is form,

that is emptiness,

whatever is emptiness,

that is form.

HEART SUTRA

To be wronged is nothing
unless you continue
to remember it.

CONFUCIUS

This above all; to thine own self be true,
And it must follow, as the night the day,
Thou canst not be false to any man.

SHAKESPEARE

Our limited self is the
wall separating us from the self of God.
It is being to self that is
the recognition of God.

HAZART INAYAT KHAN

All life is an experiment.

OLIVER WENDELL HOLMES

Ask and it shall be given unto you.
Seek and it shall be given.

LUKE 11:9

The only lasting beauty is the beauty of the heart.

RUMI

The highest wisdom is loving kindness.

THE TALMUD

The Spirit of the Buddha
is that of great loving
kindness and compassion.

THE BUDDHA

Very little is needed to
make a happy life.
It is all within yourself,
in your way of thinking.

MARCUS AURELIUS

Accustomed long to
contemplating Love
and Compassion,
I have forgotten all difference
between myself and others.

MILAREPA

In your own house dwells
the treasure of joy;
So why do you go begging
from door to door?

The disciplined man masters
thoughts by stillness
And emotions by calmness.

LAO TZU

The longer I live the more
beautiful life becomes.

FRANK LLOYD WRIGHT

Do not seek the truth
stop having an opinion.

SENG-T'SAN

Mankind's role is to fulfill his heaven-sent purpose
through a sincere heart that is in harmony
with all creation and love all things.

MORIHEI UESHIBA

Everything flows on and on
like this river, without pause,
day and night.

CONFUCIUS

How can I be still,

By flowing with the stream

LAO TZU

Underlying great doubt there is great satori,
where there is thorough questioning
there will be thorough going
experience of awakening.

ZEN SAYING

Awaken the mind without fixing it anywhere.

DIAMOND SUTRA

Not Knowing how near the truth is,
People seek it far away, what a pity!
They are like him who
in the midst of water,
Cries in thirst so imploringly.

HAKIUN

If we walk

The true Way

In our inmost heart

Even without praying

God will be with us!

TAKUAN

If we wish to die well we,
must learn how to live well.

HIS HOLINESS THE DALAI LAMA

Hampton Roads Publishing Company

. . . for the evolving human spirit

Hampton Roads Publishing Company publishes books on a
variety of subjects, including spirituality, health,
and other related topics.

For a copy of our latest catalog, call (978) 465-0504 or
visit our distributor's website at *www.redwheelweiser.com.*
You can also sign up for our newsletter and special offers by
going to *www.redwheelweiser.com/newsletter.*